Ask God
Anything!

Ask God Anything!
Esther Bailey

Illustrated by Mike Kazybrid

Scripture Union

First published 2002

Scripture Union, 207–209 Queensway, Bletchley, Milton Keynes,
MK2 2EB, England.
Email: info@scriptureunion.org.uk
Website: www.scriptureunion.org.uk

ISBN 1 85999 395 8

Scripture quoted from the Contemporary English Version © American
Bible Society. Anglicisations © British and Foreign Bible Society 1996.
Published by HarperCollins*Publishers*. Used with permission.

British Library Cataloguing-in-Publication Data. A catalogue record of this
book is available from the British Library.

Printed and bound in Great Britain by Creative Print and Design (Wales)
Ebbw Vale.

*Scripture Union is an international Christian charity working with churches in
more than 130 countries, providing resources to bring the good news about Jesus
Christ to children, young people and families and to encourage them to develop
spiritually through the Bible and prayer.*

*As well as our network of volunteers, staff and associates who run holidays,
church-based events and school Christian groups, we produce a wide range of
publications and support those who use our resources through training
programmes.*

Contents

How to find your way around the Bible

In *Ask God Anything!*, we use the Contemporary English Version (CEV) of the Bible. It is an ideal modern version for children and adults too. But use your own Bible, whatever the version. Finding your way around the Bible can be a bit of a puzzle. We can't give you the page numbers for the readings. So if you're stuck, look at the Contents page at the front of your Bible.

On page 22 you are asked to read Matthew chapter 6 verse 26.

Each book of the Bible is broken up into chapters. There are 28 chapters in Matthew's gospel. This reading comes from chapter 6.

Each chapter is split again into verses. You'll be reading verse 26. The verse numbers in the Bible are usually very small.

Esther introduces herself

Hello! Who are you? I know you must be a person of great taste, because you've chosen to pick up this book. (You did choose to pick it up, didn't you? I wouldn't like to think of you sitting there being forced to read this!) I wish I could know more about you: what sort of music you like, your favourite food/colour/TV programme, what you really think about school, what you spend your spare time doing and what's important to you.

It isn't very easy for me to get to know you, but I could tell you a bit about me, so you know where I am coming from.

I'm the mother of two children who are younger than you – at the moment Abigail is six and Joanna is two. My husband John loves fiddling round with computers, but I only like computers when they do what they are supposed to. I like Abby's computer games though!

I was born on a Thursday – have you heard of the saying "Thursday's child has far to go"? Well, when I was six weeks old, my family caught a boat from Southampton and went to live in Africa. I only returned to live in England when I was 23.

I love to see animals in the wild. I get just as excited about badgers and deer in this country as elephants, giraffe and buffalo in Africa. My favourite place in the whole world is Victoria Falls. It is so beautiful! If ever you get the chance, you must go and see it!

I used to work for Scripture Union, going to visit Christian clubs in schools. Some of the groups were similar to B Club 6, the club in this book. Now I edit a magazine giving teachers ideas for R.E. lessons.

I grew up in a Christian family. My parents taught me a lot about how to live God's way and the importance of finding out more about God through the Bible. Now that I have my own family, I want to point them to God in the same way my parents pointed me. In fact, I get a real buzz out of helping anyone get to know God better, which is why I've written this book. I hope you enjoy it!

Esther

Meet B Club 6

Perhaps you come from a family that goes to church, perhaps you don't. Perhaps you know a lot about God, perhaps you don't. Perhaps you call yourself a Christian, perhaps you don't. The question is, why should you, living in the twenty-first century, read the Bible?

Let's meet the members of B Club 6 at St Peter's Primary School to discover their opinions, difficulties, positive ideas and thoughts about the Bible.

B Club 6 is a group that meets once a week during lunchtime to read the Bible together. 'B' stands for 'Bible' and '6' means Year 6, because at the moment the club is only open to Year 6 children. It only started this term, and Kate's mum who runs the club wants to see how it goes before opening it up to other year groups.

Kate's mum →

First of all, there's Kate. Kate is in a bit of a dilemma. She feels that she should go along to the club and support her mum, but she also feels that she already knows a lot of the Bible stories, so it could be quite a waste of time.

The biggest problem with the Bible is that it's so boring! The writing is so small that it's hard to read. Also it puts me off because the pages are so thin. It takes me a long time to get the right page.

Kate ⟶

Leila is Kate's best friend. Secretly, she's thrilled that the club has started because she has wanted to try to read the Bible for a while – although how uncool that would be to admit to anyone! Leila feels sure that if she reads the Bible, she will find out more about God.

For me, the most difficult thing is telling everyone that you want to read the Bible. People just laugh!

Leila ⟶

Carl goes along to the group because there's nothing much else to do at lunchtime. Besides, it's warmer indoors than out on the playground! He is beginning to wonder, though, whether having to read the Bible might be too high a price to pay for staying inside.

> The thing that puts me off most is I don't understand how reading the Bible can make you a better person!

Carl ———▶

Ben's gran goes to church and she gave him a Bible when he was christened. He's tried reading it but found it very hard. He would like to know more about God, because his gran often talks about God, and Ben really likes his gran.

> I think it's hard trying to understand all of the old words. It puts me off because sometimes I don't know what's happening.

Ben ———▶

Kate had been hoping that Matthew would come along to B Club 6. Matthew goes to the same church as her and is extremely fanciable! However, Matthew can't come to the club because it clashes with football practice – he's the school's star striker.

> For me the most difficult thing is finding time to read the Bible! I want to read it because I know it will help me to live the way God wants me to, but when?!?

Matthew ⟶

Esther

I used to visit a lot of primary and middle schools, and at one stage, I did a mini-survey to find out whether or not children are still interested in the Bible these days. I was very surprised to discover that in every school I visited, there were some young people who had picked up a Bible and started reading it at the beginning. (That probably isn't the best way to read the Bible, at least not at first. The Bible is like a library of 66 separate books. You wouldn't walk into a library, pick up the book nearest the door, read that, put it back, read the next one, etc. You look for something you like from the library, and in the same way you need to find suitable things from the Bible.) The point was, that in spite of all the reasons not to read the Bible, these young people felt that there might be something of interest to them in there.

Your say

What about you? Have you ever tried reading the Bible? Why? What would you hope to get out of reading the Bible? What things have put you off?

1) I tried reading the Bible from the start but it put me off.
2) I tried reading the Bible because I wanted to know what people did. 3) I would hope to find good verses in the Bible. 4) All the hard words put me off the Bible.

Bible bits

How to use the Bible

When she started the group, Kate's mum suggested they each got hold of a modern translation of the Bible. The school has a set of Good News Bibles, so that's mostly what the group used.

Your say

Do you have a Bible? What version is it? If you're getting a new one, you could look at a Good News Bible, like the children at B Club 6 used, or a Contemporary English Version Bible (CEV for short) – quite a new translation, and very easy to use. All the Bible verses in this book are from the CEV Bible.

I was really surprised when I saw how different the school Bibles were from mine. Sometimes it just didn't seem the same at all! But even though the words are easier to understand in the school Bible, I still don't always get what it's on about!

Ben

You can get hold of notes to explain the parts you don't understand. Our youth worker at church is always going on about different things we can get to help us.

matthew

Matthew's right – a number of Christian organisations produce Bible reading notes for people your age. Scripture Union has *Join in – Jump on!* for 5- to 7-year-olds, *Snapshots* for 8- to 10-year-olds and *One Up* for 11- to 14-year-olds. You can also get the Bible on a CD ROM. This makes it very easy to find out all that the Bible says on a particular topic, because the programme will search for any word requested and give a list of all the verses that include it. There are also notes that explain some of the difficult-to-understand passages – you just have to click on the words that need to be explained.

Kate and Leila are discovering the benefits of reading the Bible in a group.

Even though I know most of what's in the Bible, it's more fun to do things together than on your own.

kate

Leila

The Bible is sort of like a torch because it shows me what I need to do now and when I'm older. It helps me decide what to do and always helps me when I'm feeling sad or worried about something.

That's an interesting thought, Leila. In fact, the Bible says something very similar about itself. Have a look at Psalm 119 verse 105.

kates.mum

Here it is: it says, "Your word is a lamp to guide me and a light for my path."

kate

Carl, however, is still not convinced!

I think the Bible's like a manual for life. You can choose to use it or not. You can decide if it's how you want to live, but you don't have to.

Carl has actually hit the nail on the head. No one can make you do what the Bible says; you have a choice. Just reading the Bible isn't the same as reading it and putting it into practice. As a man called James wrote in the Bible: "If you hear the message and don't obey it, you are like people who stare at themselves in a mirror and then forget what they look like as soon as they leave. But you must never stop looking at the perfect law that sets you free. God will bless you in everything you do, if you listen and obey and don't just hear and forget." You can find this in James chapter 1 verses 23 to 25. (The 'message' and the 'perfect law' are other ways of talking about the Bible.)

Esther

As I grew up, I found that having people to explain parts of the Bible was a great help. I was lucky enough to have parents who read the Bible. They helped me read it and understand it. I went to a children's church group and that helped, although it also gave me a lot of questions about what I was reading. I had to think things through for myself. When I went to secondary school, I went to the school's Christian club (a bit like B Club 6 – there wasn't one at my primary school). We talked about parts of the Bible together and with the teacher who led the group. I found that there were books and notes to help people my age understand more. I think it's really important to find help, otherwise it's very easy to give up reading the Bible. In Acts chapter 8 verses 27 to 31, we read about a man who was reading part of the Bible. When someone asked him whether he understood what he was reading, he replied, "How can I understand unless someone helps me?"

Your say

What ways of reading the Bible have you
discovered? What has been most helpful?
Have you tried putting what you read
into practice? How has that gone?

1) I use snap shots that
helps me understand.

2) I use to do Joini p Jump
on they where a lot of
help.

3) I haven't put what
I read into practice.

4) I think is I did it
it would be very good
because is you where
in trouble you could
remember a vise.

21

How can the Bible help me?

What might encourage you to read the Bible? Perhaps remembering a time when the Bible helped you? Or maybe realising that it can teach you something about how to live your life? Or even understanding that it can help you get to know God?

Some of the Year 6 pupils are feeling worried as they think about going to secondary school next September. At B Club 6, Kate's mum challenged them to find something in the Bible to help when they are worried.

Kate and Leila borrowed Kate's mum's concordance. A concordance looks a bit like a dictionary, with long lists of words in alphabetical order. After each word there's a list of all the verses in the Bible that contain the word. They looked up the words 'worry' and 'worried'. As Kate and Leila looked through the lists, they found a verse each that they thought would help when they felt worried.

In Matthew chapter 6 verse 26 it tells us that God takes care of the birds, so he will look after us. We're worth much more to God than the birds. I'll try to remember that when I'm worried.

Kate

We don't have to be worried because in John chapter 14 verse 1 Jesus says: "Don't be worried! Have faith in God and have faith in me."

Leila

Ben went to ask his gran what she does when she feels worried.

Ben's gran: One of my favourite verses is John chapter 3 verse 16: "God loved the people of this world so much that he gave his only son, so that everyone who has faith in him will have eternal life and never really die." If God loves us enough to give his own son for us, he will do anything for us, so I don't need to worry.

Carl made a point of finding Matthew for a chat.

> What do you do when you are feeling worried, Matthew? Have you ever read anything in the Bible that could help?

carl

matthew

> When it seems like everything is going wrong, I remember Romans chapter 8 verse 28: "We know that God is always at work for the good of everyone who loves him."

After the group had reported back their discoveries to Kate's mum, Leila asked her whether she ever felt worried about things, and what she thought about to help.

Kate's mum: I do get worried about all sorts of things, and all the verses you've discovered are ones that help me too. When I'm really worried, I think about times in the past when God has helped me, and I read stories about him helping other people in the Bible. I know that God doesn't change, he's always the same. He can still do all the wonderful things that he's done before, and that helps me to "have faith in him", as Leila's verse said. In Psalm 118 verses 5 and 6 it says, "When I was really suffering, I prayed to the Lord. He answered my prayer and took my worries away. The Lord is on my side, and I am not afraid of what others can do to me." That sounds like a positive attitude that I want to copy.

Esther

I find that different parts of the Bible are helpful at different times. When I was going through a very hard time, I found the story of the storm on Lake Galilee helped me (Luke chapter 8 verses 22 to 25). Although we know that Jesus calmed the storm, the disciples didn't know that would happen. But they were comforted because Jesus was with them in the storm. I didn't know how my 'storm' would work out, but I did know that Jesus would be with me through it.

Your say

What sort of things make you worried? What do you do about it? Would any of the verses that B Club 6 found help you? Choose the verse that you find most helpful and write it out neatly onto a piece of paper. Draw a border round the verse and then stick it up somewhere that you will notice it often (such as in the corner of your bedroom mirror.) Tell God about the things that worry you and ask him to help you.

① It makes me worried when my car breaks down.

② Call the A A

③ Leila's verse will help me the most.

John ch 14 V1

B Club 6's favourite Bible bits

Year 6 had been asked to write a book review for homework, so the members of B Club 6 were thinking of writing about things they have read in the Bible.

Kate: I've enjoyed reading all about David. I like the bit where David beats Goliath with just one stone – was that in 1 Samuel chapter 17? He was only a child and he didn't have any armour, but he trusted God. I like this story because it shows if you really want to do something, even if it's very difficult, you can do it if you trust in God.

Carl

I didn't think I'd like any of the Bible, but that was a good story. It's about fighting and I like watching fights! WWF is the best! David wasn't scared and was brave all the way through.

Ben

My gran told me that she reads the Ten Commandments every day for guidance. One of those psalms that David wrote says that God will instruct us and guide us. "You said to me, 'I will point out the road that you should follow. I will be your teacher and watch over you.'"

Kate's mum: Well done, Ben, that's Psalm 32 verse 8. Have you read the Ten Commandments yourself? You can find them in Exodus chapter 20.

Leila: There was loads of stuff in Psalms, wasn't there? I wrote some of the verses down when we read them, because I liked them. What we read in Psalm 68 verse 6 could help if you're feeling lonely: "You find families for those who are lonely." If you're afraid, remember what we read in Psalm 46 verses 1 and 2. "God is our mighty fortress, always ready to help in times of trouble. And so, we won't be afraid!"

I agree, Leila. I think the Bible offers lots of help when we're feeling low. Jesus tells his disciples in John chapter 14 verse 1, "Don't be worried! Have faith in God and have faith in me."

Kate's mum

Later, Kate met up with Matthew and asked him whether he had any favourite parts of the Bible. Matthew had to think hard before answering.

Matthew: Do you remember that memory verse we had at church last week? Micah chapter 6 verse 8. It says, "The Lord God has told us what is right: 'See that justice is done, let mercy be your first concern, and humbly obey your God.'" That's one of my favourites because it tells me how to live. If I'm not sure what's right, I read the verse my mum wrote in the front of my Bible when she gave it to me. Proverbs chapter 3 verses 5 and 6: "With all your heart you must trust the Lord and not your own judgment. Always let him lead you, and he will clear the road for you to follow."

Kate: Those sound quite heavy. What do they mean?

Matthew: I want to live God's way, but I know that it's very difficult. The verse from Micah tells me what God expects, but the second verse tells me how he will help me live up to that, because otherwise I wouldn't be able to.

Esther

When I was a teenager, one of my favourite verses was Psalm 119 verse 9, which says: "Young people can live a clean life by obeying your word." That verse encouraged me to keep reading my Bible, so that I would know what God's word was.

One of my favourite Bible characters is Gideon (Judges chapters 6 and 7). When an angel comes to tell him that God has chosen him to rescue God's people, Gideon is convinced that it's a mistake or a joke. He doesn't feel he's the stuff that heroes are made of. But God does use him, and Gideon realises that without God, he can't do anything, but with God, he can do whatever is needed. There are plenty of times when I need to remember those two things!

Your say

Do you have a favourite part of the Bible, a story or a verse? Have any parts of the Bible ever helped you? If you do find something helpful, how can you make sure that you don't forget it? Do you know anyone who reads the Bible? Why not ask them what their favourite verse is?

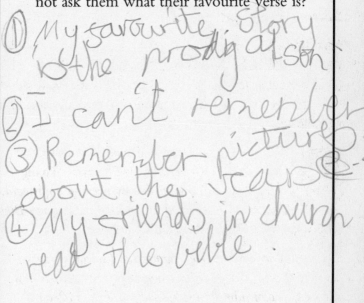

1. My favourite story is the prodigal son

2. I can't remember.

3. Remember pictures about the years.

4. My friends in church read the bible.

Prayer bits

Esther

When I was growing up, we used to read the Bible every day as a family. We would discuss it a bit and then we would all take turns to pray out loud. Every day, I would pray more or less the same thing: "Dear God, thank you for the good day we've had today; please bless my family and all my friends; and please forgive me for all the wrong things I've done today. Amen." I wasn't very satisfied with this prayer, but I had got stuck into a rut and I was too embarrassed to try anything else in front of my family.

Your say

Have you ever tried praying? Was it easy or difficult to find words to say? Have you prayed on your own, or with other people, or both? What sort of things have you tried praying about? *Helping people Healing people who are sick. Help MdS knangs*

32

How should I pray?

At B Club 6, Kate's mum has been
suggesting that the group pray about the things they
are reading in the Bible.

Kate's mum: Prayer is talking to God and
listening to what God says to us in reply.
We can pray about anything, any time,
anywhere. A good way to pray is to do it
while you are reading your Bible. Before you start
reading, pray something like: "Lord God, please help
me to understand what you are saying to me through
your word today." Some people use a verse such as
Psalm 119 verse 18 as a prayer: "Open my mind and
let me discover the wonders of your Law." Read the
Bible, then think about what the passage is saying. Is it
teaching you something new about God? Is it saying
something about the way you should live? Is it
reminding you of the things you need to thank God
for? Is there a warning there? When you have thought
about what God is saying to you, then you can talk
back to him, like a conversation. You may want to say,
"Lord God, I don't understand this. What does it
mean?" You may want to thank God for something, or
say sorry about something. You may want to tell God
about something that makes you angry or sad. You
may need to ask for his help. All of these are types
of prayer.

Leila

Don't you have to use all sorts of special words when you pray – things like 'Amen' and stuff?

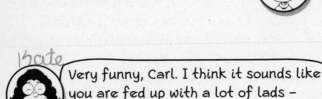

Carl

What does 'Amen' mean? It doesn't really make sense, does it? It should be 'A-man' or 'some-men'. And that's a bit sexist!

Kate

Very funny, Carl. I think it sounds like you are fed up with a lot of lads – 'Aaaah, MEN!!!'

Kate's mum: Yes, it does sound strange to us. That's because it isn't an English word – it's from the Hebrew language. You don't have to say 'Amen', but people often use it at the end of a prayer to mean 'so be it', 'this is true', or 'this is what I believe'. Sometimes other people join in, repeating 'Amen', to show that they agree with what has been said, and they are making it their prayer too.

Lelia

I sometimes feel embarrassed to pray because I can't think of very much to say.

Kate

Well, I suppose it's like when we're talking. Sometimes there's loads to say; other times we just say a couple of words, but we're still comfortable thinking together.

Ben

My gran is always talking to God. She says it doesn't matter how much you say, God just loves to hear from you.

Carl: Matthew took me to meet his youth leader the other night and he gave me a book called *Snapshots*. It's great because there are some notes that explain the passage to you. Sometimes there are some questions to think through or a puzzle to do, and an idea for how to pray or what to pray about. It's really good fun.

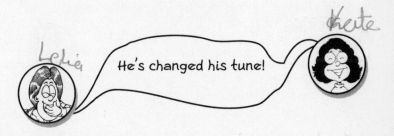

Lelia

He's changed his tune!

Kate

It's a good idea to keep a list of things that you've prayed about. I have a friend that I pray with every week and we write down the things that we've prayed about. Over the years we've noticed that God has always answered our prayers. Sometimes he says "yes" quite quickly and then we remember to say "thank you". Sometimes he says "no" and sometimes he shows us why he has said that, but sometimes he doesn't. We have had to trust that he knows best. Sometimes he has said "wait", so we've kept on praying and eventually the answer has come. Sometimes he's had to say to us, "You are praying the wrong way about that thing. You're looking at it from your point of view, not from my point of view" and so we've had to learn to look at things differently. Over the weeks we've found that our prayers for that thing have changed. Sometimes God tells us to do things to answer our own prayers! What we have noticed, though, is that God always listens to our prayers and answers them.

As you read prayers from people in the Bible, one thing you'll notice fairly quickly is that they are all absolutely honest with God. Whether they are feeling good or bad, angry or sad, they don't just pretend to God that everything is okay. They tell him exactly how they are feeling, and then allow God to show them how he is working in that situation. We should be honest when we talk to God, too. He knows exactly how we're feeling anyway, so it's a bit silly to pretend otherwise!

Your say

Have you ever talked to God about what you have read in the Bible? Has God ever answered any of your prayers? How? Have you ever told God what you really feel about something (whether that is positive or negative)?

Why not try keeping a list of things you are praying for? Get a notebook and draw a line down the middle of each page. On one side of the line write the date and the things you are praying for. Fill in the other side when God answers your prayers.

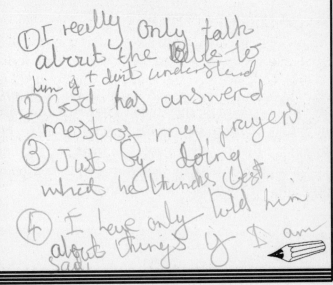

①I really only talk about the Bible to him & + dan't understand
②God has answered most of my prayers.
③Just by doing what he thinks best.
④ I have only told him about things if I am sad!

B Club 6 talk to God

After listening to Kate's mum's advice, the members of B Club 6 decided to have a go at telling God how they felt about the things they had read in the Bible. They made their prayers into a poster. Leila, who has the neatest handwriting, wrote out Psalm 18 verses 1 and 2 and stuck it in the middle of a sheet of poster paper.

I love you, Lord God, and
you make me strong.
You are my mighty rock,
my fortress, my protector,
the rock where I am safe,
my shield, my powerful weapon,
and my place of shelter.

Then everyone wrote prayers on post-it notes and stuck them all around the poster. At first they all wrote short prayers, because they didn't know what to write, but as they began to get into it, they wrote more. No one except Ben put their names on their prayers, but that didn't matter because God knew who each one was from and what each one was about.

Dear God,
Thank you for helping me when times are rough for me.
Amen.

Dear Lord,
Please help the poor and those who are ill.
Amen.

Dear God,

Please look after me.

Amen.

Dear God,
I pray that you
will be my rock
when things are
difficult and hard!
Amen.

Dear God,
please let
Grandpa know
you're with him.
Love from Ben.

Dear God,
Please help my mum's
mum and dad because
they're quite weak and
tired from looking after
everybody.
Amen.

Dear God,
Please be a rock for the people who don't know you, or are coming to know you. Please, Lord, be their rock.

Dear Lord,
Thank you for sticking with me in difficult times.
Amen.

Thank you, God, that I've known you in difficult times and that I know you will always be there for me and never abandon me.

Dear God,
Thank you for helping me when times are hard. Thank you for your love.
Please help me to get better at not doing things that my friends drag me into, being naughty and doing things I don't want to do.
Amen.

As they looked at their post-it notes, the group realised that some of the prayers were thanking God for things that he had already done for them, and some were asking for his help. Some of the asking was for themselves and some was for other people. It was interesting to see the different sort of thoughts that came from reading something written thousands of years ago!

Your say

Read the verses from Psalm 18 again. Do you agree with the writer's descriptions of God? What would you want to say to God in response to these verses? Why not try making your own poster using these verses, similar to the one B Club 6 made.

B Club 6 write prayers to God

One week the group decided to write a prayer together. They had been reading a story in the Bible about a man called Jacob, who had such a big fight with his brother that the brother wanted to kill him. Jacob had to run away from home. As he ran, Jacob realised that he couldn't run away from God, and in fact God made him a promise in Genesis chapter 28 verse 15:

"Wherever you go, I will watch over you."

Everyone spent some time thinking about God's promise, then they passed a piece of paper round the group and each person just wrote one line. This was the finished prayer:

Dear God,

Please watch over me wherever I am and wherever I go. Thank you, God.

Please watch over me at home.

Please watch over me at school.

Please watch over me when I go on holiday.

Please watch over me when I'm scared.

Thank you for watching over me and thank you for helping me, Father.

Amen.

On another occasion, Kate's mum asked them each to think of something about God that really puzzled them and to write it down as a prayer. Nobody showed their prayers to anyone else, so that they could be completely honest with God and not be afraid that anyone would laugh at them.

Ben wrote:

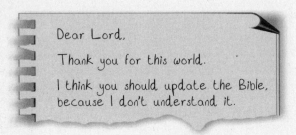

Dear Lord,

Thank you for this world.

I think you should update the Bible, because I don't understand it.

Kate was very glad that no one else saw what she wrote:

Dear God,
I don't get why you made me because I am just bad and sometimes I don't believe in you.
Love from Kate xxx

Carl spent a long time writing and this is what he came up with:

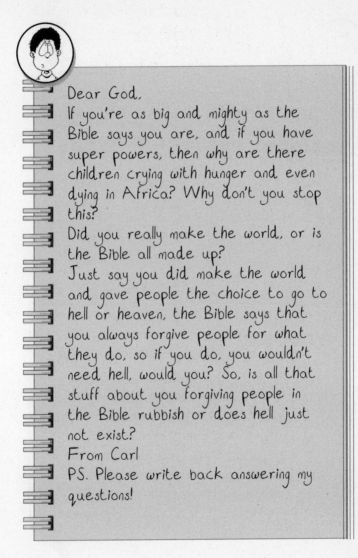

Dear God,
If you're as big and mighty as the Bible says you are, and if you have super powers, then why are there children crying with hunger and even dying in Africa? Why don't you stop this?
Did you really make the world, or is the Bible all made up?
Just say you did make the world and gave people the choice to go to hell or heaven, the Bible says that you always forgive people for what they do, so if you do, you wouldn't need hell, would you? So, is all that stuff about you forgiving people in the Bible rubbish or does hell just not exist?
From Carl
PS. Please write back answering my questions!

Leila finished very quickly because she knew exactly what she wanted to write:

Dear God, it's kind of you to die on the cross, but why? Yes, I know you love us, but do you really love _me_?

Your say

What do you think about B Club 6's prayers? Are you puzzled by the same sorts of things as they are? What would you have written if you had been there that day? Write a prayer telling God the things about him that puzzle you. Perhaps you could show the prayer to someone (an adult Christian, maybe?) who could help you understand more?

B Club 6's thank you prayers

At the end of term, B Club 6 had a 'thank you shout'.
They stood in a circle and took turns to say 'thank
you' prayers to God. Leila was worried that someone
else would start talking at the same time as her, so Ben
suggested that they passed a beanie baby around the
circle. If you had the beanie you could say something,
if you didn't want to say anything, you just passed the
beanie on to the next person. No one could quite
believe how long the 'thank you shout' went on for!
The beanie baby kept on going around and around the
circle as the group kept on thinking of more and more
things to say thank you to God for!

Dear God,
Thank you for everything you have done for people – the food and air you have given us. Help us to look after people and animals. Amen.

Dear God,
Thank you for all the great things you have done for us, for example, loving us, caring for us and all the other stuff you have done for us. Thank you.
Amen.

Dear God,
Thank you for technology and medicine which help us to learn and build things.

Dear Lord,
Thank you for making the sun, wind and rain.
Thank you for everything.

Dear God,
Thank you for all the things you have done for us; giving us homes and families and giving us food and drink.
And thank you for letting us decide what to do and make our own decisions.
And thank you for giving us such brilliant friends and family.
Amen.

Dear God,
Thank you for making our world and making my mum and dad. Please could you look after my family and friends.
Also thank you for all of our stuff.
Thanks once again!
Amen.

Dear Lord,
Thank you for making people and earth and placing us here. Thank you, Lord, for the sky, wind and rain and thank you for the teachers and mums and dads. Thank you for my life.
Thank you!
Amen.

Thank you, God, for helping me when I am worried and upset.
Thank you, Jesus, for making me.
Thank you, Jesus, for loving me.
Amen.

Dear God,
Thank you for the things you have given me. You have given me eyes so I can see, a nose that I can smell, a mouth so I can talk and ears so I can hear, a heart so I can live and lungs so I can breathe, hands so I can feel and feet that I could walk.
Amen.

Dear God,
I'm just saying thank you for everything you have done for us like feeding us and keeping us healthy. Thank you for everything. We love you!

Thank you for creating lots of
wonderful things.
Thank you, God, for all the animals and
plants. Thank you for my life.
Thank you, God, for all my friends.
Thank you for healing my neighbours.

Thank you for healing people.
Thank you for helping the poor.
Thank you for everything.
Thank you, God, for forgiveness.
Thank you, God, for the Christians who share
their love for Jesus with their friends.

Dear God,
I want to say thank you for animals,
friends and the earth.
Thank you for our families and other
people who help us.

Dear God,
I like you!
Amen.

That last prayer was from Ben and sounded so funny that everyone just started laughing and laughing, and, instead of passing the beanie baby on again, Ben just threw it up into the air. Thinking about so many things to thank God for had made everyone feel really great!

Your say

Do you agree with some of the things that B Club 6 thanked God for? What would you have said? Spend some time making a list of all the things that you want to thank God for. Have you included things that they didn't think of?

A prayer to say sorry

Matthew: Sometimes, when I read the Bible, I realise that I'm not living the way God wants me to. Then I have to say sorry to him, which is quite hard to do. It's worth it though, because God promises that whenever we say sorry to him, he will forgive us. It's such a relief to say sorry and then know that I can be close to God again.

Matthew's right – when we do things that are wrong or forget to do the right things, it's like there's a barrier between God and us. God doesn't want that barrier there, because he loves us. So whenever we say sorry, he is more than ready to forgive us. In 1 John chapter 1 verse 9 it says: "But if we confess our sins to God, he can always be trusted to forgive us and take our sins away."

Here's a prayer you might like to say to God if you're sorry about something:

Dear God,
Sorry for the things I've done wrong. Please help me to live in a way that makes you happy. I'll try my very best, but I will also need your help. Thank you for everything you have done for me.
Amen.

Your say

Have you ever said sorry to God for things that you've done that weren't right? What did you feel like before you prayed? Did you feel any different afterwards? Is there anything that you need to say sorry to God for right now? Sometimes it helps to write down the things that you have done wrong, say sorry to God and then tear the paper up. Tearing the paper up helps you to remember that God has forgiven you, so you don't have to keep on feeling bad about things you have done.

What about becoming a Christian?

Ben went to talk to his gran about prayer.

Ben: Gran, do you ever pray to God?

Gran: Oh yes, I talk to him all the time! I like to praise him and tell him how great he is. I say sorry to him for all the things that I do wrong, because I know those wrong things make him sad. I ask him to help me when I'm worried about something, I talk to him about decisions that I need to make and I thank him for all the things he has done for me.

Ben: But why do you talk to God so much?

Gran: Because I'm a friend of God's, a member of his family. Long ago, when I was about your age, I told God that I wanted to live his way. I said that I was sorry for all the wrong things that I had done and I thanked him for sending Jesus to take the punishment for those wrong things. I asked God to give me the power to do what was right, not what was wrong. That's called 'becoming a Christian'. Since I became a Christian, I've tried to read the Bible nearly every day, because through the Bible, God tells us how we should live. I've also kept on praying, talking to God about everything.

Ben: Can anyone become a Christian?

Gran: Yes! Anyone who wants to live God's way and is sorry for the wrong things they have done can become a Christian at any time.

Your say

Are you a Christian? If so, how did you become one? Have you ever told anyone about it?

If you have any questions or if you want to know more about becoming a Christian, ask an adult that you know is a Christian. If you want to, write to me at Scripture Union, 207-209 Queensway, Bletchley, Milton Keynes MK2 2EB.

Questions, questions...

Esther and questions

My two-year-old daughter is full of questions. She wants to know, "What are you doing?"; "Where are we going?"; "Why?"; "Why?"; "Why?" My six-year-old daughter has lots of questions, too. She wants to know where things come from, how things work, why things are made the way they are made and lots, lots more. It's natural to ask questions — that's how we find out things and learn about our world.

Sometimes people think, "I can't believe in God because I have too many questions". Other people think, "I believe in God, so I can't have any questions — otherwise people would think I don't believe any more!" I'm not sure that either of those is right. Everyone has questions about life, but I think that learning more about God and reading more of the Bible will help us to understand more. Of course, we will never understand everything! There will always be questions — that's because we are only people and not God! But if we honestly look for the answers to our questions, it will bring us closer to God.

As B Club 6 started thinking more and more about God, all sorts of questions started bubbling out of them! Kate's mum tried to answer some of them, but some of the questions were things that she didn't completely understand herself! God is so much greater than people are, and so people will never understand everything there is to know about him.

Your say

Here are some of the questions that children like those in B Club 6 asked. Are any of these things that you have been wondering about? What do you think of the answers – are they helpful or do they raise more questions? Do you have other questions that are not tackled here? How can you think these through?

B Club 6's questions about God

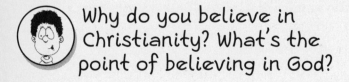 Why do you believe in Christianity? What's the point of believing in God?

I think that, at some time in their lives, everyone has questions like "Who am I?" "Why are we here on earth?" "Why is earth here?" "What happens when we die?"

For me, believing in God means that I'm not just an accident that happened to occur. I was made for a special purpose — to love and serve God. That gives me a great sense of security. Whatever happens in my life, I know that God is always with me, he loves me and he wants me to live for him.

Does God really have a son?

God is a bit like a family with three members. Each member is different, but each one is completely a member of the family.

When God's son, Jesus, came to earth, he was completely God, but that didn't mean that there was no God anywhere else. There was still God the Father and God the Holy Spirit.

One helpful way of working out the difference between the different members of "the God family" is to think of God the Father as the one who made the world; God the Son as the one who saves us and makes us able to be God's friends, and God the Holy Spirit as the one who is always with us and helps us to live God's way. The confusing bit is that all three "family members" are part of one God and all three have always existed! How amazing is that?!

(Although we talk about God the Father, that doesn't mean that God is a man. God is like a perfect parent. He has all the best characteristics of ideal fathers and ideal mothers rolled into one!)

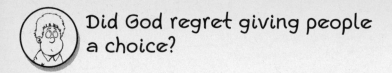 Did God regret giving people a choice?

When God made people, he could have made us like robots that were programmed to obey him without question. Instead, he gave us the choice of whether to live his way or not. We call this free will.

I don't think God regrets giving us free will. Allowing us to choose means, of course, that many people will choose not to follow him. However, I think God feels that the joy of having some people choose to love him because they want to, not just because they have to, is worth all the pain of those who reject him.

One summer, I borrowed a friend's glove puppet for our holiday club. Whenever I picked up that puppet, it did exactly what I wanted it to do – it opened its mouth and 'talked', it waved to the children, it cuddled me, it told stories, it looked happy or sad whenever I wanted it to.
It was great!

My two-year-old daughter is just learning to obey me. Sometimes she does exactly what I want; sometimes she lies on the floor, screaming and kicking her heels, and sometimes she just does exactly what she wants and ignores me. Occasionally I think it would be much easier just to have a puppet!

But I only had the puppet for a week in the summer, and would fairly soon have got bored with it. Although I sometimes find Jo difficult, I love her and will never be bored with her. When she does choose to try to please me, I become a typical boring mother – thrilled, delighted, proud and sure that my child is the best in the whole world.

In the same way, God is hurt and sad when we choose to ignore him or to disobey him, but absolutely thrilled when we choose to love him, serve him and live his way. In fact, Luke chapter 15 tells us that even all the angels in heaven celebrate when even one person turns to him!

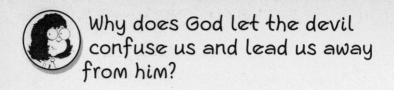

Why does God let the devil confuse us and lead us away from him?

The devil is God's enemy. He is not nearly as strong as God, and he was totally defeated when Jesus died on the cross. He knows that he's already lost the battle, but the devil is trying to hurt God in any way he can. He knows that God loves people so much that he would do anything to save them, so the devil's major tactic is to try to turn people away from God.

The devil is very deceitful and it's easy to believe him and his lies. However, we have a choice. Each of us has a conscience that tells us what's right and what's wrong. The more that we feed our conscience with God's words, the stronger it will become and the harder it will be for the devil to fool us. Philippians chapter 4 verse 8 tells us to "keep your minds on whatever is true, pure, right, holy, friendly and proper. Don't ever stop thinking about what is truly worthwhile and worthy of praise."

Of course, if we do turn away from God, we can always go back to him, say we are sorry and start again. God can always be trusted to forgive us and take our sins away.

How do I know God loves me?

The Bible is always telling us how much God loves us. In Psalm 23, King David draws a word picture of God being like a loving shepherd, with us as his sheep. God provides everything that we need: food, drink, protection, rest, direction and security. In verse 6 David says, "Your kindness and love will always be with me each day of my life."

King David was very aware of God's love, but we have even greater proof of God's love for us, because of something that happened about a thousand years after David had died. God became a person, Jesus, and died on the cross so that we could become friends with God. In 1 John chapter 4 verses 9 and 10 we read, "God showed his love for us when he sent his only Son into the world to give us life. Real love isn't our love for God, but his love for us. God sent his Son to be the sacrifice by which our sins are forgiven."

God will continue to love us whether or not we love him in return. He will be overjoyed if we do love him, and sad, hurt or even angry if we choose not to love him, but he will always love us. In Romans chapter 8 verses 38 and 39 it says, "I am sure that nothing can separate us from God's love – not life or death, not angels or spirits, not the present or the future, and not powers above or powers below. Nothing in all creation can separate us from God's love for us in Christ Jesus our Lord!"

One of my favourite songs says:

"I'm special because God has loved me,
for he gave the very best thing that he had to
save me;
his own Son, Jesus, crucified, to take the blame,
for all the bad things I have done.
Thank you, Jesus, thank you, Lord,
for loving me so much.
I know I don't deserve anything;
help me feel your love right now
to know deep in my heart
that I'm your special friend."

If Jesus cured so many sick people with the touch of his hand then why doesn't he come down and help others who are dying of serious diseases?

This is a really difficult question. Most of us know of someone who is ill. Some people are prayed for and they get better, but some people are prayed for and they still die.

Jesus healed a lot of people while he was here on earth. But even he didn't heal everyone who was ill at that time. He was healing people to show that he was a loving God, not to become popular or famous.

Nowadays, even though Jesus isn't physically here with us, we can still pray and ask him to heal people. Sometimes people are healed miraculously, sometimes they aren't. Sometimes people say that through their illness they have learned a lot more about God than they would have done if they had been healed.

If people are cured, they'll perhaps get ill again and eventually die. The healing was only postponing what would happen anyway. However, Christians believe that when we die, everyone who's said sorry to God and accepted Jesus, goes to be with God forever in a place where there is no more pain, sadness or illness. In Revelation chapter 21 verses 3 and 4 it says, "God's home is now with his people. He will live with them, and they will be his own. Yes, God will make his home among his people. He will wipe all tears from their eyes, and there will be no more death, suffering, crying or pain. These things of the past are gone for ever." For some people it is far better to go straight there, than to have to carry on living in this world where there is still death, suffering, crying and pain.

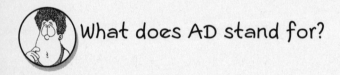 What does AD stand for?

AD stands for the Latin words 'anno domini' which means 'in the year of our Lord'. Jesus' birth was such good news for the whole world that we now number years from that time. The years before Jesus was born are known as AD (before Christ) and years afterwards as AD. However, this method of counting the years was worked out about 500 years after Jesus was here on earth, and it seems that mistakes were made. Jesus was probably born sometime between 12 and 5 AD!

B Club 6's questions about the Bible

What do you like about the Bible?

The Bible reassures me that God is always with me, that he always loves me and he is always ready to forgive me. It tells me that he has a plan for the world and that he is powerful enough to work things out, even when they are in a terrible mess. He will sort things out fairly.

One of the things I like about the Bible is that it helps me realise how great God is. As I read the Bible I see him at work in lots of people's lives. God never changes; so I know he is still the same today as he was back then.

Something else that I like about the Bible is that it shows me how to live if I want to please God. It gives me guidelines, but it also shows me how far I fall short of God's standards.

I'm confused about the Bible. Some of it is weird. Why should I read it?

The Bible wasn't written as a storybook for young people to read. It was written by people whose cultures are very different to our own, so it's not always easy to read or understand. But it's important to read the Bible because through it, we discover what God is like and how he wants us to live. As we read the Bible, think about what it says and try to put it into practice, God's word will change our minds and make us more like him. Try reading Matthew chapter 13 verses 3 to 9. Jesus said that God's word is like a seed in our minds. It could just disappear like seed eaten by birds if we don't think about it, it could just be squashed out by all our other interests, like plants that are squashed by weeds, or it could grow and grow and make us more like God, like a plant producing many more seeds.

B Club 6's questions about living as a Christian

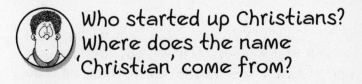 Who started up Christians? Where does the name 'Christian' come from?

Jesus started up Christians. Christians are people who believe that Jesus is the son of God and that he died to take the punishment for all the wrong things we do, so that we can be friends with God. The name 'Christian' started off as a nickname in a town called Antioch. People noticed that the people who believed in Jesus were always talking about 'Christ' (another name for Jesus), so they called them 'Christ-ians'. It was meant to be a mocking name, but Christians are proud to be named with Jesus' own name and so the nickname stuck.

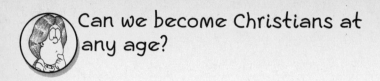
Can we become Christians at any age?

Yes, we can. The first person to become a Christian was a man who was dying. He was on the cross next to Jesus and he said, "'Remember me when you come into power!' Jesus replied, 'I promise that today you will be with me in paradise.'" (Luke chapter 23 verses 42 and 43) Some people became Christians so young that they can't remember a time when they weren't God's friend. Whatever age you are, if you're not already a Christian, God says, "That time has come. This is the day for you to be saved."
(2 Corinthians chapter 6 verse 2)

What happens if we become Christians but then do and say wrong things? Do we have to become Christians again?

Good question! Lots of us start off full of enthusiasm, wanting to live God's way and not do any more wrong things. Pretty soon though, we find that we're struggling to keep it up. "I don't understand why I act the way I do. I don't do what I know is right. I do the things I hate. Even when I want to do right, I cannot. Instead of doing what I know is right, I do wrong." Does this sound familiar? That's what Paul wrote in Romans chapter 7 verses 15, 18 and 19. All of us get it wrong. All of us make mistakes. What we need to do is to say sorry to God, then he will give us a new start. 1 John chapter 1 verse 9 says, "If we confess our sins to God, he can always be trusted to forgive us and take our sins away." So we don't need to become Christians again every time we make a mistake, but we do need to say sorry to God.

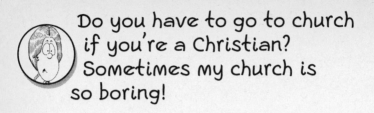

Do you have to go to church if you're a Christian? Sometimes my church is so boring!

Have you ever watched a fire? All the individual pieces of wood and coal glow and burn fiercely when they are grouped together. But if one piece falls away, it gradually cools down, changing from white to red to black, and stops burning. One of the main reasons for going to church is to keep you in touch with lots of other Christians, so that you can encourage each other and keep each other 'burning' for God. It's much harder to stay 'hot' as a Christian on your own. In Hebrews chapter 10 verses 24 and 25 it says, "We should keep on encouraging each other to be thoughtful and to do helpful things. Some people have got out of the habit of meeting for worship, but we must not do that. We should keep on encouraging each other, especially since you know that the day of the Lord's coming is getting closer."

That's fine, but what if you are the only one doing any encouraging? What if no one is encouraging you, and you're just getting bored? In that case, I think you have two options. Option one: you may be able to go to another church, where you will get more help. However, if that's not a possibility, you will have to try option two: decide that you will go to church to spend the time remembering and thanking God for the things he has done for you. As you sing the hymns, look at the words – what do they tell you about God or Jesus? As you listen to the prayers, listen out for phrases describing what God has done. Read the Bible passage, look at the service book, listen to what is being said, and find something to praise God for. It might be hard work at first, but if you ask God to help you worship him, he will!

When I first started teaching, I was living in a little town that had very few Christians. I went to a church with about 12 members, all at least 30 years older than me. It was very different from the big, lively church I had left. The church asked me to start a Sunday school, which I did. Soon we had a number of children from the school I taught at coming to church and Sunday school. I was encouraging those children to live for God, but I was concerned because no one was encouraging me. I prayed about it. Then someone told me about a group of nurses who were having Bible studies at the hospital on Monday nights. I went to investigate and found a group of lively, encouraging people who were able to help me live God's way. God had answered my prayers.

Why are there so many different churches?

Have you ever moved schools, or visited another school? I expect you have found that there are some things that are common to every school, but also some things that are in one school, but not in another. Some schools have a reputation for being good at sport, some are better at music and drama, some get excellent SATs results. However, there are still plenty of features – such as teachers, books and lessons that help you recognise that it's a school and not something else.

In the same way, there are lots of different types of churches that place emphasis on different things. But there are things that are common between all churches.

In Acts chapter 2 verses 42 to 47, we learn that the first church were like a family to each other. They met together to learn about God, to praise God, to pray, to break bread together and to share meals. They shared everything they had with each other.

As the church spread around the world, and more people from many different cultures joined the church, different groups developed different ways of doing things. Today we see branches of the church that have formed in different areas – the Coptic Church in Ethiopia, the Russian Orthodox Church, the Greek Orthodox Church, Roman Catholics and even the Church of England and the Church of Scotland.

As years went by, some of the churches developed more and more rituals. Every now and then, a group of people would say, "This is too formal, we want to get back to the simple ways that the first Christians used to worship God." So they would break away from the main church in a country and form a new denomination – Methodists, Baptists and Presbyterians all started in this way.

Although denominations started in many different ways, today there is much variation between churches, even within the same denomination. But the people in all of the denominations are "like a building with Christ as the most important stone. Christ is the one who holds the building together and makes it grow into a holy temple for the Lord."

B Club 6's questions about heaven

Do animals go to heaven? Can pets go to heaven?

One of the differences between people and animals is that people have souls but animals don't. This means that people can be aware of God and can worship him – all human tribes and nations have some form of religion, but no animals do! When we die, our bodies die, but our souls continue to live. When animals die, I'm afraid they just die. This means that when we go to heaven, we won't be able to meet up again with specific animals that we have known and loved. However, the Bible tells us that God is creating a new heaven and earth that will be so wonderful that no one will even remember this old earth any more. (Isaiah chapter 65 verse 17). Since animals are such a wonderful part of this world, I'm sure that there will be animals in the new world that God is making, and that they will be even more amazing than the ones we have known and loved here.

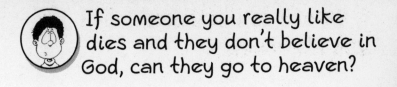 If someone you really like dies and they don't believe in God, can they go to heaven?

This is a really difficult question, but I'll have a go at answering it!

The Bible tells us that God is so pure and holy that nothing that does any wrong can go anywhere near him. If you put your hand on a hot stove, you can't help but scream and pull your hand away. So it is with God: anything bad can't help but scream and run away from him. All of us do wrong things or think bad thoughts, so none of us would be comfortable in heaven, close to God.

This creates a really big problem for God, because he loves people and wants them to live with him in heaven forever. That's why Jesus became a person and died: "But God showed how much he loved us by having Christ die for us, even though we were sinful." (Romans chapter 5 verse 8). If we believe in Jesus, say sorry to God and ask him to forgive us for the wrong things we do, then we belong to God, and "anyone who belongs to Christ is a new person. The past is forgotten, and everything is new." (2 Corinthians chapter 5 verse 17). It's only because we believe in Jesus and God has made us new that any of us can go to heaven. If we had not believed, we would still be in the state where we could not go near God, because of our badness and his pure goodness.

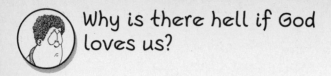 # Why is there hell if God loves us?

God didn't make hell for people. Matthew chapter 25 verse 41 tells us that it was prepared for the devil and his angels. However, 1 John chapter 3 verse 8 tells us that, "anyone who keeps on sinning belongs to the devil." We do keep on doing wrong things, and so we deserve to be punished with the devil and his angels. But, as you say in your question, God does love us and doesn't want any of us to be punished. That's why Jesus came to die on the cross – he didn't have to, but because he loves us, he came to take the punishment we deserve. Now we all have a choice: we can ignore what Jesus did, or we can say sorry for the wrong we do, thank him for dying for us and ask him to help us live his way. The second option is called becoming a Christian, and if we do that, God will wipe out all the wrong things we have done and we will belong to him.

When we die, will we ever come back to life?

When a conker falls down from its tree in autumn, the outer shell cracks off, dies and starts to rot. The conker inside continues to live and grow, and if conditions are right, could eventually become another chestnut tree. When we die, only our bodies really die, and they are buried and eventually rot away! However, our invisible soul – the part of us that can recognise God – doesn't die. What happens to it depends on whether we have asked Jesus to forgive us for all the wrong things we have done. In John chapter 3 verse 16 it says, "everyone who has faith in him (that's Jesus) will have eternal life." If we've asked Jesus to forgive us and put our faith in him, our souls will live with him in heaven for ever!

B Club 6's other questions

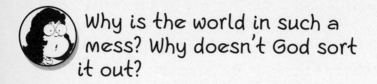 Why is the world in such a mess? Why doesn't God sort it out?

When God first made the world, it was perfect! In Genesis chapter 1 verse 31, we read that, "God looked at what he had done. All of it was very good!" God's plan was that the people he had made would look after the world. In Genesis chapter 1 verse 28, God tells people, "Rule over the fish in the sea, the birds in the sky, and every animal on the earth", and in Genesis chapter 2 verse 15, we read that God "put the man in the Garden of Eden to take care of it and to look after it.". But people are selfish! Some people use the world and other people to make more money or power for themselves. This is why the world is in such a mess.

So, why doesn't God sort it out? Well, his plan still is for people to sort it out. He wants us to recognise our responsibility. When we turn to God and start loving him, we start to see things his way. We care about looking after the beautiful things he has made. We start to realise that all people are important to God, even those that are poor, homeless and weak. We begin to understand that if God has given us lots of good things, we need to share what we have with others.

Well, you may ask, what does that mean to me? What can I do? Maybe you won't be able to stop the rain forest being cut down, or to provide food for all the hungry people. But you could decide to give a portion of your pocket money to organisations that do try to put God's plans for the world into practice. You could think about not being greedy, and only use as much as you really need. And what about recycling waste paper, glass and aluminium? It may not feel like you are doing much, but if everyone did something, we would make a big difference.

I once heard a story about a beach where thousands of starfish had been washed up by the high tide and stranded on the sand. A man walked down the beach picking up starfish and throwing them back into the water. Someone watching asked him why he was wasting his time. There were so many starfish dying on the beach that one man throwing a few back wouldn't make any difference. The man picked up another starfish, and, as he threw it back into the sea, he said, "It makes a difference to this one."

We can't change the whole world, but we can make a difference to individuals. We sometimes feel sad because the problems of the world are so big. God can deal with big problems, because he is even bigger and greater, but we should also remember that he knows each person in the whole world by name and he cares about the problems that each one has. He wants to use us to help sort things out.

You know how Elijah stopped the rain? Do you think God could give me the power to stop the rain in Britain, because I would like that a lot!

There's a man in Acts chapter 8 who thought he could buy God's power for his own convenience! He had been using witchcraft to amaze people, so they gave him the nickname 'The Great Power'. He became a Christian and gave up his magic tricks. He was fascinated by the miracles that Philip was able to perform in God's power, but then Peter and John arrived. When Simon the ex-magician saw Peter and John placing their hands on people and the people receiving the Holy Spirit, he was totally stunned. He brought some money to Peter and said, "Let me have this power too!" Peter told him off very severely for thinking that he could buy God's gift!

God does have the power to stop the rain in Britain, but he probably wouldn't use his power in that way. God doesn't just pull dramatic stunts so that everyone is awed. He's not an entertainer, nor does he have to prove himself to people who may or may not believe in him. In the Bible, miracles are usually used to deepen people's faith.

I used to teach in Zimbabwe in Africa. One day the children in my Christian group at school came to me and said that some of the local people were going to a mountain nearby to pray to their ancestors for rain. I asked what the children thought about that. Did they think that the ancestors could provide rain? They were very sure that only God could provide the rain, and they said, "Why don't we pray for rain, and ask God to send it before the trip to pray to the ancestors, so that everyone will know that rain comes from God?" I was a bit nervous about this. I believed that God could send the rain, but what would happen if he didn't? It's entirely up to God to decide what he wants to do; we can't force his hand. Anyway, we all prayed and kept on praying as we waited to see what would happen. A few days before the people were due to go to the mountain to pray to the ancestors for rain, we had a fun day for our school Christian group and the groups from three other schools. Usually in Zimbabwe it's very easy to plan these sorts of day outside, because the weather is so predictable that you don't need to think of wet weather alternatives. While we were in a big field doing games and drama and all sorts of activities with no shelter around, the heavens opened and it poured! It rained and rained and rained. We were drenched! All the other groups thought it was a total disaster, but my group and I were so happy and excited. God had sent the rain, and it had come before the people had prayed to the ancestors. We did some dancing in the rain that day, I can tell you!

The questions included in this book are all ones that have been asked by children and young people I know. Some of them are Christians, trying to live God's way; some of them had never seriously thought about God, but all of them have very real questions. Perhaps some of the questions are things that you have been wondering about too. If so, I hope you find the answers helpful. Perhaps some of the answers will raise more questions for you, or perhaps you already have more questions that we haven't tackled here. Whatever your question, do think it through, and ask people for advice. If you want to, write to me at Scripture Union, 207-209 Queensway, Bletchley, Milton Keynes, MK2 2EB.

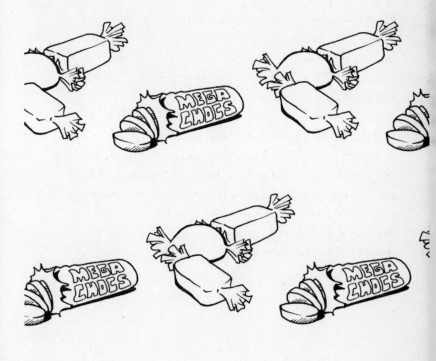

Esther says thank you

Thank you for reading this book – I hope you've found it helpful.

Of course, B Club 6 doesn't really exist; all those children, and even Kate's mum, are just people that I made up. BUT all their comments, prayers and questions really were said by actual living, breathing human beings.

Thank you very much to Y6 at WASPS, Bath; Y6 at Southdown Junior, Bath; Luke Out at St Luke's Church, Bath; and my nephew and niece, David and Ruth. All of your comments, opinions, prayers and questions were very helpful. I really appreciated your honesty.

Notes

Notes

If you've enjoyed this book, why not look out for...

Snapshots

Lively, simple and easy to use with 8 to 10-year-olds, Snapshots gives the young independent Bible reader a daily passage from the Bible, a thought, a brief activity or puzzle and a prayer suggestion. Snapshots is biblically-based and inexpensive enough for children's workers to buy for their whole group or club. Available quarterly.

Let the Land Breathe
Helen Parker

Steven cares about the caravan site where he lives with his family. When the owner of the site falls ill, an unscrupulous developer tries to take over; Steven feels like David against Goliath as he fights to let the land breathe. A fast-paced adventure with a strong environmental theme, which also shows that you can trust God for everything.

ISBN 1 85999 543 8

Seasiders: Angels
Kathy Lee

Grace is always trying to go 'the extra mile' for people, but chasing art thieves and run-away mothers was never part of the bargain! And what will happen if it gets dangerous? Will there really be an angel around to help?

Angels is the fifth book in the popular Seasiders series. Each book features a complete story about the residents of a seaside town.

ISBN 1 85999 445 8

All of these titles are available from
Christian bookshops, or online at
www.scriptureunion.org.uk/publishing
or call Mail Order direct on **01908 856006.**